Hawk Mother Returns

A STORY OF INTERSPECIES ADOPTION

KARA HAGEDORN
MARLO GARNSWORTHY

Web of Life
CHILDREN'S BOOKS

One spring morning, my phone rings. Someone has cut down a tree with a nest containing two red-tailed hawk eggs. "Will Sunshine adopt them?" asks the **wildlife rehabilitator**.

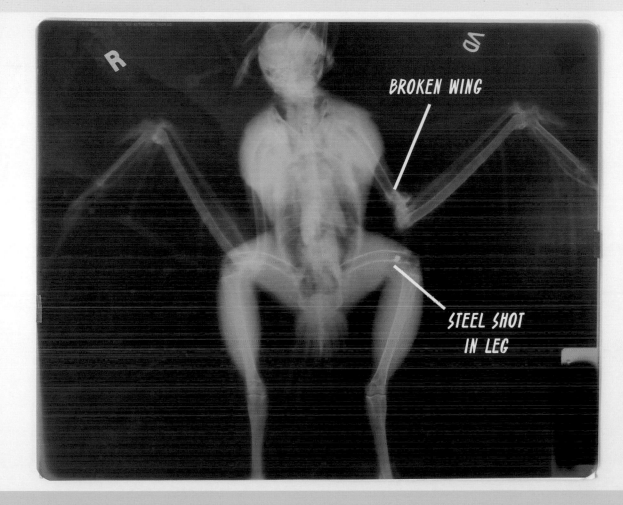

Sunshine the red-tailed hawk has been unable to fly since she was shot many years ago. Because I am a **zoologist**, I am allowed to take care of her. I named her Sunshine because of her bright personality.

Each spring, Sunshine built a nest. Then she laid two eggs. Because they were **infertile**, the eggs never hatched. It made me sad that a human took away her freedom to fly, find a mate, and raise young. But one year, I had an idea.

I gave Sunshine two **fertile** chicken eggs. In the wild, the chickens would be **prey**. But Sunshine's **instinct** to be a mother was so strong that she raised them to adulthood!

That was a few years ago. Because Sunshine successfully adopted eggs before, I'm confident that she can raise the hawk chicks.

"Sunshine, some eggs are on their way!" I say. Sunshine hops outside, plucks some rosemary, and begins to freshen her nest.

But when the eggs arrive, one has already hatched into a fuzzy gray chick!

When I compare the other egg to a larger red-tailed hawk egg, I realize these are the **offspring** of a red-shouldered hawk. Will Sunshine accept the egg and newly hatched chick of a competing hawk **species**?

When Sunshine leaves to stretch under the willow trees, I carefully place the fluffy gray chick in Sunshine's nest. I listen to the faint peeping from inside the egg and settle it beside its sibling.

Sunshine hops from perch to perch up to her nest. "Look, Sunshine! Look!" I cry. "You have a chick!" Sunshine peers at the chick and egg in wonder. She looks up at me. "Could it be?" I feel her thinking.

I hold my breath as she gently strokes the chick's head with her beak. And then she carefully rolls the egg beneath her and snuggles up to her chick. She **preens** its long, downy feathers. When she tucks sprigs of rosemary around its small body to keep it warm, I decide to name the chick Rosemary.

Every four hours, I bring Sunshine small bits of meat. Rosemary wobbles and stares up at Sunshine with a wide-open mouth. As Sunshine feeds her, the chick's **crop** puffs out until I'm sure it will burst! Then she falls over happily and stumbles under Sunshine to snooze.

While Sunshine feeds and **broods** Rosemary, the egg slowly cracks. The chick's **egg tooth** breaks through the shell, cutting its path to freedom. An hour later, a wet, exhausted chick has hatched. I name her Bella. Sunshine nudges Bella up against Rosemary, and the new family settles down for the night.

Sunshine's hooked beak is built for tearing, and she offers little pieces of meat. Both chicks are big eaters! Sunshine dotes on them, hardly ever leaving their side. Most of the time, they sleep, snuggling with Sunshine or each other. When they're awake, they watch their mother's every move!

Although I want to cuddle and talk to the chicks, I watch from a distance. It's critical for hawks to **imprint** on their parents, so they understand they are hawks. If they have no fear of people, they rarely survive in the wild. So, I wait until the chicks are a few weeks old before I pick them up to weigh them and check their health. Sunshine isn't worried. She has known me a long time and trusts me completely.

At three weeks old, Rosemary and Bella's gray down has thickened. Their cloudy eyes have cleared. They sit up, turn, and poop off the edge of the nest to keep it clean.

Sunshine feeds them bigger pieces of meat. The chicks can eat bones now. Any undigested fur or feathers form a **pellet**, which hawks spit out every couple of days. As the chicks move about more, Sunshine builds up the sides of the nest with sticks to protect them from falling out. But mostly, they just want to snuggle.

After four weeks, Bella and Rosemary are in a full **molt**. Their striped black-and-white tails reveal that they are definitely red-shouldered hawks.

The chicks watch Sunshine preen and **mimic** her. They make soft clucking sounds. When they are older, they will make the loud cries—*Kee-aah! Kee-aah!*—red-shouldered hawks are famous for.

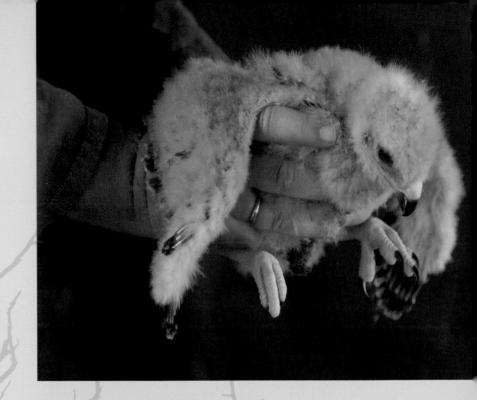

At five weeks, Rosemary stands for the first time but quickly grows tired. Bella watches, and then she stands, too! Now that they can stand, Sunshine starts hunting lessons.

Sunshine scans the **aviary** floor for wandering grasshoppers, lizards, and snakes. She hops from perch to perch, patiently waiting, while the chicks watch.

Sometimes Sunshine eats the prey away from the chicks. The chicks wobble to the edge of the nest. "Hey!" they chirp. "What about us?" But Sunshine knows she is encouraging her chicks to fly.

At six weeks, Rosemary hops to a nearby perch then flutters farther away to a stump. Bella watches Rosemary flit from perch to perch, and then she too makes the leap. The chicks have **fledged**! They use their **talons** to grasp the food and their sharp beaks to tear it into pieces and feed themselves.

One day, I notice that Rosemary
is smaller than Bella. Since male
hawks are smaller than females,
I realize he is a male and change
his name to Romeo.

The **fledglings** become stronger fliers, and they're catching mice on their own. I know it will soon be time for them to leave. Their biggest challenge will be hunting prey. In the wild, hawk fledglings often return to the nest area to beg for food. I want Romeo and Bella to feel safe to stay around here if they want.

I decide today is the day for them to leave. I take Sunshine out of her aviary so she can watch.

Then, heart beating, I open the aviary door. I assume Romeo and Bella will high-tail it out of there. But they don't. They stay high on their safe perches.

I try to flush them out. Eventually, I put on thick gloves and catch Bella. Then I step out into the sunlight and release her.

"Ah!" I breathe with wonder as Bella spreads her striped black-and-white tail, circling above, wild and free.

Romeo wants nothing to do with me. He hops around the aviary until he finds the door. Romeo flies out and lands on a pine branch. Then he soars south toward the forest.

Bella flies off, too, but she swoops down to join Sunshine the following afternoon. From then on, Bella visits her mother every few days.

Sunshine teaches Bella all she knows. She scans the ground and catches wild gophers and snakes while Bella watches. She eyes a passing turkey vulture, making sure it's not a dangerous golden eagle. By returning to her aviary at sunset, she warns Bella to find a safe night **roost**.

Bella will eventually leave home, like all juvenile raptors do. I will miss her and Romeo. It was the careless actions of humans that hurt these hawks. But it was also the love and care of Sunshine and me that saved their lives. Though Sunshine will never fly again, her adopted chicks will live wild and free, just as they are meant to be.

I'll always remember how Bella and Romeo brought us together in this **interspecies** adventure of mothering and healing. I'm so grateful for the trust and understanding I share with my friend Sunshine, the Hawk Mother.

Bella and Romeo's Story Continues

Bella continued to visit Sunshine for over a year. The next year, Bella built a nest in a large nearby tree. She raised at least twelve chicks over four years. They hunted and learned to fly in the field beside Sunshine's aviary. Later, Bella moved to a nest down by the creek, and I lost track of her. Red-shouldered hawks still fly into the yard. I'm pretty sure they are Bella's offspring. Exactly one year after I released him, Romeo landed on the roof above me! I recognized him immediately by his petite body and gray-green eyes. He stayed about an hour until Bella chased him off. I have never seen him again, but I hope that he and Bella are still raising chicks and living happily, wild, and free.

Kara and Sunshine

Because of my degree in zoology and my experience working at the Cornell University Hawk Barn, I qualified for the necessary permits to become Sunshine's caretaker. I'm guessing she was around three years old when I adopted her because she had the red tail of an adult but the pale-yellow eyes of a juvenile. I made a serious commitment to care for her, knowing that hawks can live for over thirty years in captivity.

Sunshine and I spend time together every day. We have learned to communicate through body language, so I can tell if she is hungry, irritated, bored, excited, relaxed, or ready to go to sleep in her aviary. Sunshine teaches me to be more patient and observant. She gives a rasping call to let me know if a cat is in the yard. She turns an eye to the sky to alert me to a golden eagle soaring overhead. Adopting Sunshine has transformed my life, and I am happy that I am able to enrich her life by helping her become a hawk mother—and more than once!

When Sunshine hatched and raised baby chickens with my help, I shared our story in the book *Hawk Mother: The Story of a Red-tailed Hawk Who Hatched Chickens*. Together we have given hundreds of presentations in schools, parks, and libraries, educating thousands of people about the importance of protecting birds in the wild.

More About Hawks

There are more than two hundred species of hawks worldwide. They live in every habitat except for the North Pole and South Pole. Seventeen species of hawks live in North America.

The red-tailed hawk is the most common hawk in the United States and Canada. It lives in open habitats, including desert, scrubland, grasslands, woodland, and even tropical rainforest. As they circle in the sky, red-tailed hawks are easily identified by their bright red tails.

Red-shouldered hawks are less common. They are smaller, with a reddish-brown chest and a striped black-and-white tail. They prefer to live in forests, near rivers or swampland. You may see either species perching on telephone poles, where they sit patiently looking for rodents, insects, snakes, and other animals to eat. While red-tailed hawks also eat larger mammals such as rabbits, hares, and squirrels, red-shouldered hawks prefer smaller prey, including amphibians and crayfish.

Some farmers call red-tailed hawks "chicken hawks" because they blame them for killing their chickens. Although hawks will sometimes kill young chickens who stray too far from the coop, chickens are more likely to be victims of a fox, raccoon, or weasel raiding their coop. Farmers sometimes shoot or poison hawks without realizing they actually help protect crops from hungry rodents and rabbits.

Today, many countries have laws to protect hawks. In the United States, all birds of prey are protected under the Migratory Bird Treaty Act. It is illegal to disturb a hawk nest or to keep hawk eggs or chicks. Unfortunately, despite these protections, many hawks like Sunshine are still illegally shot, or chicks like Bella and Romeo are left homeless. To find out more about hawks and how you can help protect them, contact the organizations listed below.

Birdlife International www.birdlife.org

The National Audubon Society www.audubon.org

Royal Society for the Protection of Birds www.rspb.org.uk

Glossary

aviary – large structure designed for birds to live in

brood – sit on eggs or chicks to keep them warm

crop – an enlargement of the gullet (throat) of a bird that forms a pouch to receive food and prepare it for digestion

egg tooth – sharp growth on the nose or beak of a baby bird that it uses to break through the shell of its egg when hatching

fertile – able to grow a baby chick inside it

fledge/fledgling – to leave the nest after growing feathers needed for flying; a young bird that has developed the feathers it needs to fly

imprint – how a baby bird learns what species it is; baby birds imprint on whichever species they interact with first

infertile – not able to grow a baby chick inside it

instinct – natural behavior an animal is born with that it doesn't have to learn

interspecies – between more than once species

mimic – to imitate closely

molt – to shed feathers, which are replaced by new feathers

offspring – the young of an animal, person, or plant

pellet – a wad of material (such as fur or feathers) that can't be digested and is regurgitated (thrown up) by a bird of prey

preen – to groom with a beak

prey – animal being hunted, caught, and eaten by another animal

roost – a resting place on something high above the ground, such as a tree branch or wooden perch

species – a group of living things made up of related individuals who are able to mate and produce offspring

talons – sharp, pointed claws on the feet of a bird of prey

wildlife rehabilitator – someone who cares for orphaned, sick, or injured wild animals until they are ready for release into the wild

zoologist – a person who specializes in the study or science of animals

To Cindy Pfost and Madeleine Dunphy, who made this book happen. ~ K.H.
To Phillipa: bestie, superhero, Hawk Mother. ~ M.G.

Text © 2024 Kara Hagedorn & Marlo Garnsworthy
For ages 5–9

Contributing Photographers: Glenn Forbes, Kara Hagedorn, Eva Vigil

Published in the United States in 2024 by Web of Life Children's Books, Berkeley, California.

Library of Congress Control Number: 2023943516
ISBN: 978-1-970039-08-5

Book design by Marlo Garnsworthy, Icebird Studio, www.IcebirdStudio.com.

Printed in China by Toppan Leefung Printing
Production Date: August 2023
Batch: 01

For free, downloadable activities, and for more information about our books and the authors and
artists who created them, visit our website: www.weboflifebooks.com.

Distributed by Publishers Group West/An Ingram Brand
(800)788-3123
www.pgw.com